GOING TO THE PICTURES

Nottingham Civic Society is an independent non-political organisation working on behalf of Nottingham's environment and quality of life.
With many other groups holding similar interests the Society supports the well-being of the city.
The Nottingham Civic Society welcomes all those interested in Nottingham's past, present and future. Further details are available on our website.
www.nottinghamcivicsociety.org.uk

First published in 2014

© Michael Payne / Civic Society

*The right of Michael Payne to be identified as the author of this work
has been asserted in accordance with the Copyrights, Designs and Patents Act 1988.*

Designed by R & J Media

*Russell Press, Russell House, Bulwell Lane,
Basford, Nottingham NG6 0BT
www.russellpress.com - www.russellpressdigital.co.uk*

ISBN 978-1-902443-12-6

GOING TO THE PICTURES

A Short History of Cinema in Nottingham
by Michael Payne
Foreword by Stephen Frears

Nottingham Civic Society

Acknowledgements

A huge debt of thanks is due to Douglas Whitworth for his generous assistance with photographs from his personal collection. This has been invaluable.

To Hilary Silvester and Ken Brand of the Nottingham Civic Society for their encouragement in devising this book.

Dorothy Ritchie of Nottingham Libraries and Information Service, Local Studies Collection.

Geoff Blackwell, Ernest Day, Terry Fry, Laurence Geary, Bob Massey, Rick Wilde & Chris Smith.

Melissa Gueneau and David Deighton of Broadway Media Centre.

Ashley Bird for his cover photograph of Broadway Media Centre and plate 58, the Paul Smith Screen.

To my son Roger for advice on all things digital and his wife Jules for her skill and patience in the design and layout of the text and photographs.

Every effort has been made to acknowledge the source of material used here. Should any error or omission have occurred if those concerned make representation, corrections will be made in any subsequent editions.

Contents

Foreword by Stephen Frears

In 1959 I went with my Mum and Dad to see *North by Northwest* at the Carlton cinema on Chapel Bar. At the same cinema I saw *Giant* and I think *South Pacific*. My brother took us all up the Ilkeston Road to see *High Noon* and *On the Waterfront*.

I saw a revival of *Gone with the Wind* at the Elite on Parliament Street, as well as *Saturday Night and Sunday Morning* and possibly *Room at the Top* which changed the world.

John Wayne died at *The Alamo* in a cinema called the Globe on the roundabout near Trent Bridge. *Oliver Twist* and *Look Back in Anger* I saw at the Savoy on the Derby Road and Norman Wisdom down at the Tudor in West Bridgford. Danny Kaye was at the Mechanics in *The Court Jester* saying, 'The chalice from the palace has the pellet with the poison - the vessel with the pestle has the brew that is true.' Years later, on *Dangerous Liaisons*, I worked with Mildred Natwick who was his partner in this routine.

There was a rather dodgy cinema, the Moulin Rouge, down from the old Theatre Royal where I saw *The Woman of Rome* and *I was a Teenage Werewolf*.

Not bad for the Fifties, but then I've spent much of my life trying to find somewhere as wonderful as Nottingham at that time. No wonder I ended up making films.

God bless Nottingham and her cinemas !

Introduction

For the first half of the twentieth century the main form of mass entertainment in Great Britain was the cinema. Going to the pictures was the leading social activity of the time. In the 1930s and 40s wherever you lived in Nottingham, or any other city, there was usually a cinema within easy walking distance. Here, for a modest ticket price, three hours of comfort and escapism, luxury and fantasy could be enjoyed. Picture palaces were meeting places of local importance, visited weekly by half the British public.

The 1930s were the golden age of cinema construction. Demand for large cinemas (with 1,000 or more seats) seemed almost unending. In this decade 20 new cinemas were built in Nottingham, 18 of which were in the suburbs. Cinema design was often adventurous and modern, with a stronger European influence than in other domestic architecture of the time. Streamlining epitomised the era which, together with flamboyant Art-Deco interiors, added to the glamour and excitement of cinema going. Neon lighting increased the blatant self-advertising of cinemas which were built for two main purposes. That of providing entertainment and making money.

This may be one reason why so many considered them vulgar and of little merit. When cinemas began to close in the late 50s and early 60s, nobody thought of preserving them as buildings of historic importance. Later, when they became bingo halls or supermarkets, the indifference increased and there was no attempt by local authorities to save them. Only now, when most of them have gone, is it realised that these once familiar buildings are worthy of study

Of the forty or more cinemas that existed in Nottingham only the Savoy on Derby Road is still operating. The others have either been demolished or put to other uses. Just three remain as Grade II listed buildings by English Heritage.

The Parliament Street Elite and the Long Row Picture House have their white faience exteriors protected, although their interiors have been lost. A third, the Capitol at Hyson Green designed by Reginald Cooper, still stands and today is in use as a church.

1. The Rio, Oakdale Road, Carlton.
Built in 1939, the Rio was the last of the pre-war cinemas. The streamlined decor by architect Reginald Cooper draws the eye to the projected image.
Later, the narrow width of the proscenium made it hard to install the wide screen processes adopted in the 1950s.

Fairgrounds, Music Halls and Shops

There was often the feel of the fairground about cinemas. The gaudy exhibitionism, the 'Greatest Show on Earth' type of advertising, all proclaimed its place of origin.

For it was at fairgrounds that cinemas began.

In Nottingham, from the end of the nineteenth century, *Living Pictures* were an integral part of the annual Goose Fair in the Market Square. At the time of the Second Boer War (1899-1902) Wadbrook's Royal Electrograph exhibited what were described as *Savage South Africa and Bio Tableaux*. These apparent actualities of the war were, in truth, re-creations shot in the north of England. So-called Boer atrocities, followed by daring rescues from behind the enemy lines, were filmed on the Yorkshire moors and shown as reality to an unsuspecting public.

2. Wadbrook's Royal Electrograph, opposite the old Exchange. c.1899.

Twigdon's Royal Electrograph was also presenting *Briton versus Boer*. Next door, Captain Payne's Bioscope had a crudely written sign announcing 'War Latest'. Such films are early examples of the cinema being used for crude propaganda purposes.

3. Twigdon's Electrograph and Captain Payne's Bioscope showing newsreels of the 2nd Boer War. c.1899

YOUR OLD FAVOURITE

Still to the Front, and "Bang Up to Date.

WALL'S **B**OER **W**AROGRAPH.

EDISON'S ELECTRIC LIVING PICTURES

All the Latest Pictures of the Boer and China War. Also fine display of Local Pictures, including "Workpeople and Girls Leaving T. Adams and Co. Stoney-street, at Dinner Time." Shown here and nowhere else.

MARKET - PLACE (Opposite South Parade)

4. Wall's advertisement. 1900

Situated opposite Market Street, Wall's had their own presentation, curiously advertised as a *Warograph*. Of special interest is the 'fine display of Local Living Pictures'.

This was one of the earliest films shot by Mitchell & Kenyon, film makers from 1900 - 1910, showing workpeople and girls leaving Adams lace factory on Stoney Street.

The two pioneers filmed crowds leaving factories, football matches or anywhere

5. Shop on Clumber Street converted into a temporary cinema.

that would provide a potential audience. As swiftly as possible the films were shown under the heading *Come and See Yourselves As Others See You*, either in fairgrounds, or as shown, in an unused shop.

Variety theatres began to include short films as 'turns' and these were reputed to have been shown at the Gaiety Palace on Market Street in about 1898. In 1901 the Gaiety changed its name to Kings. The proprietor, Frank McNaughton, advertising it as the *Original Picture Show of Nottingham*. After renovations, Kings reopened as the Scala in 1913 which survived under various names until 1984.

7. (Below) The Scala exterior, Market Street in the 1950s.

6. Interior of the Scala showing its origins as a music hall.

Other reports claim that the Grand Theatre at Hyson Green also showed films from July 1898. Earlier, in 1886 the Grand had opened with much optimism as a rival to Lambert's Theatre Royal in Nottingham's city centre; it never succeeded as a theatre probably being too far out of town. For a period in the 1920s it became the Compton Repertory Theatre which also did not last. In 1925 it became a full time cinema.

8. The Grand Theatre c. 1922. In the centre on the other side of Gregory Boulevard can be seen the Boulevard, a cinema that opened in 1910. Both the Grand and the Boulevard closed in 1956 and are now demolished.

The Bioscope was also used educationally, with illustrated talks particularly popular.

In February 1906 at the Albert Hall, F. Ormiston-Smith Esq. gave a Grand Bioscopic Lecture on Mountaineering. His programme including film of *An Ascent of Mont Blanc, Avalanches, Falling Rocks and Snow Cols* together with scenes of skiing.

Only two months later, the Albert Hall was destroyed by fire. Although not connected, such hazards were often due to the highly inflammable film catching fire and was one reason for the introduction of the Cinematograph Act of 1909. This legislated for strict safety during the exhibition of films, ruling that projectors

ALBERT LARGE HALL,
NOTTINGHAM.

Thursday Evening, 22nd Feb.

GRAND

Bioscopic

- Lecture

ON

"MOUNTAINEERING

Its Pleasures, Dangers, and
Difficulties "

BY

F. Ormiston-Smith, Esq.
The well-known Mountaineer.

SYLLABUS.

Some reasons for Mountaineering—Climber's equipment—An Ascent of Mont Blanc—Club Hut Life—The Jungfrau—Zermatt and the First Ascent of the Matterhorn—The Gorner Grat Railway—The Ascent of Europe's Grandest Mountain, The Matterhorn—A day in the life of a Climber—A Panorama from the Schreckhorn—Dangers of the Alps—Camping out—Avalanches—Snow Cornices—Arêtes, Rock Faces and Falling Rocks—Snow Cols—The Finsteraar-joch—Grindelwald—A Comparison of Summer and Winter—Winter Sports—Ski-ing—Skating—Tobogganing and Sleighing—Conclusion.

Note—Heavier type denotes Bioscopic Illustrations.

GEORGE WIGLEY, Esq., J.P., will preside.

9. *Albert Hall Lecture, February 1906.*

must be housed in fireproof areas, completely separate from the public, a stipulation that is still in force.

Another early cinematic innovation was Hale's Tours of the World, 'offering trips to the Colonies and many parts of the World (without luggage)' [1].

It was the invention of George C. Hale, a fire chief of Kansas City, USA and for a time was a worldwide success.

In 1907, an unidentified shop on Long Row became a showcase for Hale's Tours.

The premises were converted into a railway carriage with a screen disguised as a window at the far end. Films taken from the front of trains were projected onto this. Painted scenery rolled past the side widows adding to the illusion of movement.

10. Hale's Tours of the World.

Admission was made at a mock railway booking office and as the spectators sat in the simulated railway carriage, the seats were made to shake with the added sounds of hissing steam and train whistles. The ride lasted ten minutes with locations on show ranging from Rugged Scotland to the Rocky Mountains of Western Canada. Programmes were said to change weekly.

However, the public quickly tired of this novelty, and by 1910 the Tours had disappeared in favour of films that told stories.

Within the first ten years of the twentieth century, the popularity of films was firmly established as more than a short-lived curiosity. The 1909 Cinematograph Act required licenses for the exhibition of moving pictures. The following year, 1910, saw the first purpose-built cinemas in Nottingham.

Note.
1. Christian Hayes: Phantom Rides, www.screenonline.org.uk

Nottingham's First Cinemas

In 1910 the Cinematograph Act came into being and three cinemas appeared in Nottingham. On 14 March 1910, Hibbert's Animated Pictures on Shakespeare Street opened; its name later changed to The Lounge. The exhibitor, Henry Hibbert, had shown films at the Mechanics Small Hall with sufficient success that he leased the former Central Christadelphian Hall and made it suitable for animated picture shows.

11. Hibbert's Animated Pictures. Shakespeare St.

'The interior of the hall has been decorated in two shades of blue with heavy plush curtains to match. A new electric light installation is provided, whilst tip-up chairs in red leather have been fixed throughout so that the complete comfort of visitors is assured. . . None but the most up to date films will be shown at the Central Hall. Every picture yesterday was clear and distinct.' [1]

The chief picture of the week was entitled *Chinese Yellow Devil*, 'the thrilling adventure of an English detective who cleverly outwits a Chinese desperado, whilst *The Rejected Letter,* the story of a music master who has joined a band of brigands and eventually rescues his lover from their clutches is equally thrilling.' [2] Six additional films completed the programme and were described as containing 'screamingly funny incidents.' Like Kings, Hibbert's cinema was the conversion of existing premises and not a new building. Only ten days later, around the corner on Milton Street opposite the new Victoria Railway Station, the first genuine purpose built cinema opened its doors.

12. Victoria Electric Palace Nottingham's first purpose built cinema.

This was the Victoria Electric Palace and its premier attraction was announced as 'a Magnificent Selection of Motion Pictures including KINEMACOLOR, the Wonder of the Day.'[3] Kinemacolor was an early two colour process. The Victoria offered continuous performances from 11.00 am to 11.00 pm. Admission prices were 6d and 3d, children half price. Before long, a corner balcony was installed which remained until the cinema closed in 1970.

Towards the end of its life in the 1950s as the New Victoria it premiered some of the best foreign films, not to be seen elsewhere. Classics such as *La Ronde* and *Monsieur Hulot's Holiday* drew good audiences. At the time of Cinemascope and the new wide screen innovations, many Nottingham cinemas were unable to project these films as intended and merely showed the letterbox format on the old screen ratio.

The New Victoria was able to show Cinemascope in its proper dimensions with full stereophonic sound. This began in 1954 with a spectacular film of the Royal Tour of Australia *The Flight of the White Heron* and soon queues were standing for such epics as *Carmen Jones* and *Three Coins in the Fountain*.

Its final blaze of glory was an appearance by Elizabeth Taylor and Richard Burton at a screening of their film version of *Dr Faustus* in March 1968. Two years later it was gone.

In November 1910 a third cinema opened in Nottingham. This was Pringle's Picture Palace on Goldsmith Street which was probably of a higher standard than the earlier two. It advertised itself as having 'elegance and comfort throughout...with superb pictures of comedies and dramas.'[4] Ralph Pringle had begun as a variety performer and then became the Northern Representative for Edisons Animated Films. Pringle's Picture Palace appears to have been the largest so far in Nottingham and had 700 seats with both stalls and a balcony. It also had a stage 24 feet (7.31m) in depth, with dressing rooms so that live entertainment could be provided. In these early days of cinema there were often variety acts on stage, with the performers hurrying from show to show at different picture palaces.

Pringle's seems to have been a great success and the *Evening News* reported that the pictures shown were of first class quality. 'They are beautifully clear and steady, particularly so the remarkably good picture story of *Uncle Tom's Cabin*...It is one of the best films we have seen and relates a surprising number of scenes of the famous book. *Love and Honour* is another capital dramatic film in which some excellent sea scenes are shown, whilst *Ruin*, an Italian drama, is a strong feature of the bill which also includes a number of humorous films...Appropriate musical selections by a well-balanced orchestra add greatly to the enjoyment of the entertainment.' [5]

13. *Pringle's Picture Palace (Left). Today, the right side of the street is Nottingham Trent University.*

When Pringle's closed as a cinema in 1941 there was a short period when it became the Little Theatre. Then followed a major change of fortune when the building was purchased by the newly formed Nottingham Theatre Trust transforming it into the Nottingham Playhouse soon to have a national reputation as one of the finest post-war regional theatres. Today the building still stands, but is used as a night club.

Finally that year outside the town centre, the Boulevard on Radford Road at Hyson Green opened just before Christmas 1910. Like Pringle's this too had a small stage 20 feet x 10 feet deep (6.08m x 3.04m) and two dressing rooms, with variety acts as part of its first programmes.

14. The Boulevard.

By 1913 the exhibitors at Goose Fair found themselves outclassed by the increasing comforts of the picture palaces so that fairground film shows came to an end that year. Inevitably World War One saw few new cinemas starting in business. In June 1914, before hostilities began, the Globe at Trent Bridge opened. In May 1915 the Pavilion (later the Plaza) opened, together with the Imperial on Wilford Road in

15. The Mechanics. Originally built in 1845, it became a cinema in March 1916.

September 1916. In the same year, (1916) the Mechanics Hall became a full time cinema, with the Hippodrome (later the Gaumont) also going over to the pictures, still silent it should be remembered. Between 1910 and 1914, Nottingham had sixteen localities where moving pictures could be seen regularly.

The main cinematic event before World War One was the opening in November 1912 of the Long Row Picture House. This became the leading cinema in town and was given full civic recognition with an official opening by the mayoress, Mrs E. Mellors. Described as the latest word in luxurious entertainment, there was a reception (including afternoon tea) for a large number of specially invited guests giving approval to this new form of entertainment.

The Picture House was built by the Provincial Cinematograph Theatres Ltd. who owned similar places of entertainment in the main towns of Great Britain. It had seating accommodation for 600 and the arrangement was that the whole of the ground floor was given over to 6d (2½ p) ticket holders, whilst the luxury of the balcony cost one shilling (5p). Entertainment was continuous daily from 1.00pm to 10.30 pm. The first programme included extracts from *The Merry Wives of Windsor* and *David Garrick*, with some special moving pictures of Nottingham.

16. The Long Row Picture House.   *17. (Right) As it is today.*

It was enthusiastically reported in the *Nottingham Evening News* that, 'the arrangement and decoration of the theatre itself are both beautiful and elaborate. The floor rises in tiers giving unobstructed views from each seat. There is a balcony arranged like a series of boxes along one side only; the other side of the theatre is handsomely wainscotted in fumed oak surmounted by four or five tapestry panels occupying the length of the theatre. The plaster decorations of the lofty domed roof is one of the most striking features of the building, and the whole colour scheme together with the imaginative system by which a soft glow is diffused over the place without a single direct light being discernible, gives a rich, soft artistic effect.' [6] The inclusion of a cafe was a major step

forward in providing a sense of occasion for the growing film-going public.

Throughout the era of silent films, the Long Row Picture House together with the Elite were the leading cinemas in Nottingham. The Picture House closed in 1930, never converting to 'Talkies'. This was the time of the emerging phenomenon of film stars such as Charlie Chaplin, Mary Pickford, Douglas Fairbanks and Rudolph

Valentino, all of whom rose from obscurity to be world famous.

Two such stars had performed in Nottingham when almost unknown. Between 1899 and 1910 Chaplin had appeared on stage in Nottingham at the Empire Music Hall.

First as part of an act called *The Eight Lancashire Lads* and in 1910 he was in Fred Karno's Comedy Troupe. Ten years later he was perhaps the best-known man in the world with films such as *The Kid* (1920). Also in 1910, another future Hollywood star was at the Empire. This was W.C. Fields then titled the *World Famous Comedy Juggler.*

He too achieved legendary status in Hollywood between 1924 - 1944, particularly as Mr Micawber in the 1935 version of *David Copperfield.*

18. Valentino. Screen Idol of the 1920s

Notes
1. *Nottingham Evening News (N.E.N):* 15 March 1910.
2. Ibid.
3. N.E.N: 22 March 1910.
4. N.E.N; 29 November 1910.
5. Ibid.
6. *Nottingham Evening News:* 5 November 1912.

A Dazzling Fairy Palace

Until 1914, France, Denmark and Italy had led the world in film production; language being no barrier for audiences in the silent era. The French were so advanced technically that they sent directors to the United States to instruct film makers there. With the outbreak of World War One this supremacy ended, leaving the USA, and Hollywood in particular, free to develop a film industry that rapidly overtook the world. By the 1920s many more film stars had arrived; names such as Lon Chaney, Clara Bow, Buster Keaton and Gloria Swanson. The demand by the public to see their films was unbounded, requiring more and bigger cinemas.

'It was in the trenches of France during World War One that plans were made for a future Super Picture House in Nottingham. A Nottingham officer, J.A. Lomax, told his commanding officer, Lt. Col. Adamson, how some of the worst slums in Nottingham, between Parliament Street and Long Row, had been cleared. Two wide new roads, King Street and Queen Street, had been created. Between them was an empty triangular site awaiting imaginative development, perhaps for a high quality picture palace together with offices and shops.' [1]
After the war Adamson, who in peacetime was an architect, visited the site with Lomax, himself the son of a Nottingham building contractor, and saw its potential. A company was formed to buy the site supported by Nottingham brewer Thomas Shipstone. Plans were submitted by the architects in September 1919 and nearly two years later (after strikes and 'difficulties') the building of the Elite was complete.

The Elite was given a ceremonial opening, this time by the mayor, the Rt. Worshipful Alderman H. Bowles, on Monday 22 August 1921 at 2.30 pm. In his address he described the complex as - 'perfectly located. This structure would seem destined to become not only a favourite place of resort, but one of the finest picture palaces in Great Britain, also with a high class restaurant and a splendid block of shops and offices. It is the very flower of modern super-cinemas.' [2].

Very shortly the building was being described as a dazzling fairy palace. 'The auditorium seated 1,500, with a huge orchestral organ specially designed "at fabulous cost", the largest of any in Great Britain which played at every performance.' [3]

A spacious foyer had rubber flooring to minimise noise. Originally the Elite boasted a central kitchen which afforded a full restaurant service to the beautifully decorated Louis XVI tea room. In addition to this there was a finely appointed Jacobean Room for lunches and dinners. Also available was a ladies' rest room and a gentlemen's smoking room, all accessible by electric lift.

19. The Elite. Parliament Street.

20. The Elite auditorium. (Above).   *21. The spacious entrance foyer. (Below).*

22. 1st Floor The Tea Room, decorated in Louis XVI style.

23. 2nd Floor. Jacobean Room for lunches and dinners.

24. 3rd Floor. Georgian Ladies' Room.

25. 3rd Floor. Dutch Room for gentlemen's smoking.

Programmes were given in continuous performance from 2.00pm. to
10.00pm. Prices of admission were 9d (4p), 1s 3d (6p), 1s 10d (9p),
2s 4d (11½p). The opening film was *Pollyanna* starring Mary Pickford,
then the biggest female star in movies, who with her husband Douglas
Fairbanks and Charlie Chaplin had sent telegrams of congratulations to
the new enterprise.

In the wake of this titan, three suburban cinemas were built in the
1920s.

The Berridge
Road Picture
House, (1920), the
Highbury (1921)
and the Mapperley
Majestic (1929).
This last named is
noteworthy, being
one of the first
cinemas designed
by Nottingham
architect Alfred
J.Thraves.

*26. Mapperley Majestic.
(Top right).*

*27 Leno's, Radford
Road. (Right).*

The Majestic was officially opened by Councillor J. Farr who declared that 'the City Council was always pleased to be associated with projects which featured the religious, social and recreational sides of their activities.' [4] He believed the Majestic would supply a need with its programme of educational value and healthy subject. It was not long before the Majestic advertised itself as the Elite of the suburbs.

1929 was also the year when sound films became fully established bringing in a boom period of cinema building with twenty new cinemas constructed from between 1930 and 1939, eighteen of them in the suburbs.

28. The Aspley / Commodore. (Left).

29 The Globe, Trent Bridge. (Below left).

Notes.
1. Nottingham Local Studies, The Elite Picture Theatre, Parliament Street. Souvenir programme, August 1921.
2. Ibid.
3. Ibid.
4. *Nottingham Journal.* 12 June 1929.

Continuous Performance

From 1933 the leading cinema in Nottingham was without doubt the Ritz (later the Odeon) on Angel Row. With the completion of the prominent new Council House in 1929, the centuries old market had been removed from the city centre, leaving an area thought by the Corporation to be in need of gentrification. Already department stores such as Griffin & Spalding and Pearsons (both on Long Row) brought

much of the better quality hoped for by the city council. By now the cinema was accepted as a respectable form of entertainment, so that a new prestigious cinema, namely the Ritz, would help raise the standing of the area and be a suitable accompaniment to the reconstructed Market Square.

30. The Ritz Cinema, Angel Row. c.1936.

Under the 1937 St James' Street Clearance Act a large area of slum properties was demolished, leaving a suitable site for such a development, as had been the case for the Elite a decade earlier.

Owned by County Cinemas Limited, the Ritz was designed by the London firm of architects Verity & Beverley, in association with Nottingham architect Alfred J. Thraves. The site was not without difficulties. The entrance on Angel Row was a mere 40 ft. (12.19 m) wide. This restricted access resulted in a long, narrow entrance foyer. In the event this proved to be a benefit as it provided an undercover space for queues to stand in bad weather. Following this a rotunda offered carpeted stairways leading to the main cinema (seating 2,426) together with a ballroom and restaurant in the lower floor.

31. The Rotunda.

THE ROTUNDA

The Ritz also had an impressive stage 85 ft. wide x 40 ft. deep (25.9m. x 12.2m.) complete with a fly tower for scenery, although this facility was never used fully. 'The dominant colours in the auditorium are gold and green; these are wedded to Chinese orange chiefly on the organ grilles. This is maintained in the carpets and curtains.' [1]

The Ritz cinema opened on 4 December 1933, with a gala occasion described by the *Evening Post* as 'reminiscent of a first night at the opera.' The deputy Lord Mayor performed the opening ceremony, accompanied by members of the city council, and other prominent city and council people.' The film chosen was *The Private Life of Henry VIII* starring Charles Laughton. Co-stars Binnie Barnes and Wendy Barrie who played two of Henry's wives were also in attendance.

32. The Ritz auditorium. Capable of seating nearly 2,500.

33. The Private
Life of Henry
VIII *the
opening film.*

'The wonderful lighting of the new theatre and the smart green uniforms set off with gold facings worn by the attendants were greatly admired. Prior to the opening, the band of the Robin Hoods gave a delightful programme of music by permission of Col. L.C.Brewill (Commanding Officer). Famed broadcaster Reginald Foort initiated the great Conacher organ which boasted 22 ranks, 205 stops, 1,500 pipes and 100 miles of wiring. At the conclusion of the evening performance the invited guests attended a reception.' [2]

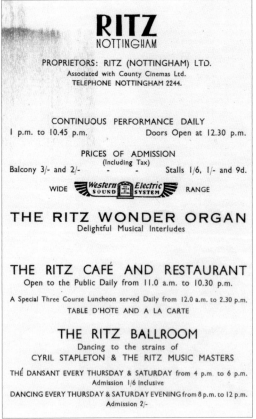

34. *Opening Programme for the Ritz.*

Stories, perhaps begun by rivals, that the balcony at the cinema was unsafe began to circulate. 'Mr Frank Verity, the architect expressed his amusement at the rumour. The steelwork of the balcony was made and installed by the same firm that built the Sydney Harbour Bridge,' he said, and was thoroughly tested by the local authorities. This comprised filling the balcony with bags of cement and then getting the army of workmen to jump up and down and hop from one step to another. When the balcony was crowded to capacity, as it was last night, there was not the slightest movement.' [3]

Dance music in the ballroom was supplied by Cyril Stapleton and the Ritz Music Masters. As a musician Cyril Stapleton had played earlier in the orchestra for silent films at the Elite. He went on to have a successful career on radio as leader of the BBC Show Band. In the 1960s, as the largest venue in Nottingham, appearances were made on stage by the Beatles, the Rolling Stones and others including the Ray Charles orchestra with Frank Sinatra Jnr.

35. The Carlton in 1949, celebrating its 10th anniversary.

Odeon Theatres gained a controlling interest from County Cinemas in 1935, but the Ritz retained its name until 1944 after which it became known as the Odeon.

Just as the Elite had attracted the city's film-going public in the 1920s, it was the Ritz that prevailed in the 1930s and 1940s as Nottingham's premier cinema. One popular part of the programme in these years was Jack Helyer, the organist who gave recitals most afternoons and evenings. Rising up into view, the great Conacher organ had a large range of sound effects from drums to bugles, whilst changing colour to suit the mood of the music. Jack Helyer devised different programmes each week with the lyrics of songs projected onto the screen for those who wished to sing along.

In 1939, the one great rival to the Ritz was built further up the road at Chapel Bar.

This was the Carlton at the corner of Mount Street, again on land recently cleared of slum housing. With a smaller seating capacity of 2,077 it still rated as a super cinema. Over the years its name changed to the 'ABC', 'MGM' and finally 'Canon'.

The Carlton was almost ready for business when World War Two broke out in September 1939. For a while the Government closed all places of public gathering.

But it was soon realised that this was bad for public morale and as

36. The Carlton auditorium.

37. The Gaumont, the last week before its closure in 1971.

the early period of the phoney war saw little enemy action, the ban was lifted. The Carlton finally opened on 16 October 1939 with *Jamaica Inn* again starring Charles Laughton. There could be no opening ceremony and the neon lighting that had been part of the external design could not be used until long after the war. Nevertheless the Carlton was described by its management as 'Nottingham's Latest and Most Luxurious Cinema'.

For two decades the Odeon and the Carlton were rivals in attracting audiences. Their fortunes were tied up with the films they were contracted to exhibit. The Odeon had rights for Paramount and Twentieth Century Fox as well as many British films.

The Carlton, owned by Associated British Cinemas, showed films made by Warner and MGM which often had the edge in box office appeal. It was perhaps true to say the Odeon was the more comfortable cinema, but the Carlton had the better movies.

Alongside both the Ritz and the Carlton was the Gaumont, formerly

38. Nightime Neon 1937. When the Gaumont was the Hippodrome.

the Hippodrome, a variety theatre that in 1927 was turned into a full-time cinema.

Built in 1906, the Hippodrome from the start had the capacity to show films and was able to accommodate an audience of 1,724 in orchestra stalls, dress circle, balcony and boxes.

It had a 60 ft (18.24 m) deep stage, that was able to mount spectacular plays that could not be accommodated at the Theatre Royal. One of these was *The Whip* which included an on-stage train crash as part of the drama.

The Hippodrome as a cinema was never fully satisfactory, its sight-lines being inferior when compared to those of the purpose built cinemas. Renamed the Gaumont in February 1948 it maintained a lead as a flagship for many famous British films of the time. First showings in Nottingham of most of the celebrated Ealing comedies were given here, as well as such classics as *Brief Encounter* and *The Red Shoes*.

Notes.
1. Nottingham Local Studies. Opening Programme for the Ritz, Angel Row. December 1933.
2. *Nottingham Evening Post.* 5 December 1933.
3. Ibid.

Suburban Luxury

Two Nottingham architects dominated cinema design in the 1930s. Alfred J. Thraves (an advisor on the design of the Ritz) started his commissions in 1929 with the Mapperley Majestic and the New Empress on St Ann's Wells Road. The latter had originated as a roller skating rink. It was thought at the start of the century that this would be a popular pastime, but the craze did not last. Victoria Hall, another large rink, had been built on Talbot Street. Thraves' next enterprise was the West Bridgford Tudor (1931).

A mock Elizabethan facade was a strange style for presenting this modern form of entertainment. Obviously the gabled appearance

39. The Bridgford Tudor.

appealed to Thraves, for he was responsible for another Tudor cinema in West Kirby. Earlier, in 1928, Thraves had been asked to design a cinema to be built in Sherwood and for this he submitted plans in his mock-Tudor style. The cinema did not materialise, but Thraves' design was utilised for a row of shops which are still to be seen on Mansfield Road above the junction with Burlington Road.

Nothing remains of the Bridgford Tudor today apart from the name Tudor Square. How many residents realise that this refers to a cinema and not to an historical period ?

40. The cinema that never was in Sherwood.

41. The Futurist, Valley Road, Basford.

Thraves continued with designs for the Dale, Sneinton and the Plaza, Trent Bridge (both in 1932). He subsequently designed the Astoria, Lenton Abbey, the Forum, Aspley Lane (both 1936), and the Futurist, Basford (1937). Thraves also designed cinemas further afield including two in Sutton Coldfield.

Reginald W. Cooper was the other dominant cinema architect of the era. His first design was the Savoy on Derby Road, Lenton (1935). In swift succession he built the Ritz Carlton and the Capitol,

42. The Capitol, now Grade II listed.

Radford (1936). The latter is listed as Grade II by English Heritage and is still in use, but as a church. In 1937 he built the Metropole in Sherwood and the Roxy in Daybrook.

The Metropole was probably his finest design, a handsome Art-Deco building which together with the Roxy is now demolished. The Adelphi, Bulwell followed in 1938 and in 1939 the Rio on Oakdale Road. Like the Carlton in town, the Rio was almost ready for opening when World War Two broke out. Completion was allowed and the Rio opened in November 1939.

Cooper's style was much influenced by Art-Deco and European architecture of the period. Three of his designs, the Sherwood Metropole, the Daybrook Roxy and the Rio on Oakdale Road, had distinctive 'fin

43. The Dale, Sneinton. c. 1932.

towers' bearing the cinema's name in neon lighting, a style far in advance of his contemporaries. One other cinema, the Ritz at Ilkeston designed by Cooper in 1938 is preserved and is now a Grade II listed building. It is sad that the Metropole especially received no protection before its demise.

The Amusements column of the *Evening Post* shows the multiple choices available for audiences in December 1954. In the 1930s, they had been considered important assets to their districts with strong support from the city council. New housing estates saw the arrival of a picture house well in advance of public houses and churches: local authorities regarding them as important social amenities.

In the town cinemas, the 'big picture' ran for a week, whereas in the suburbs there was a change of programme midweek, unless it was a major attraction when that too ran for six or seven days. The Odeon had

44. *The Metropole, Sherwood.*
45. *The foyer to the balcony.*

46. Amusement Guide. Some of the 39 cinemas in Nottingham Dec. 1954.

continuous performances from 10.00am which allowed four complete shows daily. During the war, the Sunday opening of cinemas was a controversial subject opposed by many on religious or moral grounds. Regulations eventually allowed Sunday openings from the mid war years when mainly old films were shown, almost as a deterrent to audiences. The popularity of continuous performance meant that queuing for admission was part of the cinema going habit. If the start of a film was missed it was quite normal to wait until the next showing, or if seats became available to see a film part way through .

How many films were never seen properly from the start ? Hence the once familiar saying - 'this is where we came in.'

Programmes lasted three hours or longer. The 'big picture' was usually 90 minutes in length with a supporting 'B' film about 60 minutes. Occasionally, if a major film ran for more than two hours, there was 'full supporting programme.' This consisted of one or two short films of variable quality. Added to this were newsreels, (British Movietone, Gaumont British or Pathe depending on the circuit) a cartoon and

47. Complete change of programme twice a week. The last bill of the Cavendish, St Ann's Wells Rd 1968.

trailers for forthcoming attractions. Some of the bigger houses included short documentaries such as the American *March of Time* or Rank's *Look at Life.* These were more likely to be seen at the News House, the small cinema on Parliament Street, where they were an essential part of programme.

Newsreels were often shared by cinemas. In the 1940s, Ernest Day, then a reel

48. *The News House. For many years the main source of visual news and current events, until it was made redundant by TV.*

winder boy at the Elite, remembered running to the Mechanics with the newsreel, which in turn was sent back by similar means. Such stories were not uncommon.

At the end of the evening performance, it was customary for the National Anthem to be played accompanied by a much worn image of the Queen. Tradition demanded everyone stand still during this, but usually there was a unseemly scramble for the exits beforehand.

Decline and Closure

In the first year after World War Two cinema attendance reach its peak. Throughout the war ticket sales had flourished until in 1946, cinema admissions in Great Britain reached 1,600 million.[1] However, in that same year BBC TV returned. Only in the London area at first, but by 1953, it was estimated that the pivotal event of the Coronation had been seen on nearly three million home television screens. The arrival of ITV in 1955 saw the medium become a new and major source of information and entertainment.

American and British film production continued at a high level, with the European film industry recovering. However, from the mid 1950s onwards, television had replaced the cinema as the medium of mass entertainment. In 1956, 15.8 million homes in the UK had a TV. Today that number stands at 27.4 million.[2]

Car ownership was also giving mobility and choice to many who had previously been cinema goers. The number of 'X' rated horror or sex films began to alienate the family audience. As can be seen from the *Evening Post* 'Amusements' column (Plate 46) a large proportion of the films on offer were of poor quality further explaining the dwindling audiences. 'Why turn out on a wet night when there was TV at home?' In addition to declining audiences, Entertainment Tax was taking one third of the box office revenue and adding to the exhibitors' problems.

Near panic caused the big studios to offer new technology in attempts to entice the public from their TV screens. 3D films were a novelty that lasted only a short time, as the necessity of wearing special glasses was not liked. Wide screen systems such as Cinemascope and Todd-AO seemed a better solution. Gigantic screens filled with colourful spectacle accompanied by stereophonic sound were hoped to get the better of small domestic black and white TVs.

49. *The Robe (1953) The wide screen arrives.*
Picture: 20th century Fox/The Kobal collection

The innovation required exhibitors to widen their screens which was not always possible due to the narrowness of many prosceniums. (See Plate 1.)

Film programming changed with the arrival of lengthy blockbusters such as *Ben-Hur* and *Lawrence of Arabia*. Audiences were offered separate performances for which they could book in advance; but still the decline in attendance continued.

Perhaps the solution was that as the screens grew larger, cinemas might pay if they were smaller. The Odeon in Nottingham was the first super cinema in the country to become 'twinned' by turning itself into two separate screens. Described as 'an entertainment centre of the future with a double choice of programme'[3] the Odeon was reinvented.

After six month's reconstruction, this brought about 'a complete break with tradition having nothing borrowed from the past...Once through the double glass doors, the patron is surrounded by a foyer of white Sicilian marble, cedarwood and vertical mirrors'.

Odeon One (the old balcony now seating 924) had 'wide-spaced, foam cushioned seating in royal blue and carpeting in gold and tan. The walls, an arc of gold glass-fibre forming vast pleated drapes up to full ceiling height with a 52 ft (15.80 metres) wide screen...Odeon Two (the ground floor cinema seated 1,450) had a similar decor. Both screens were equipped with giant projectors for 35mm and 70mm gauge films. Six track stereophonic sound is channelled through a range of speakers behind the screen.'[4]

50. The new Odeon foyer. 'Sicilian marble, cedarwood and mirrors.'

51. The Odeon twin screens (1965).

The Odeon Twins opened with a gala performance (not quite up to the 1933 experience) with the Lord Mayor attending a supper party before seeing a movie.

For a time this seemed to work. *The Sound of Music* ran at Odeon 1 for over two years. But films of this popularity were scarce and the fall in audiences continued, reaching its lowest level in 1984 at 55 million admissions. Social habits, especially with the young, were changing. The music revolution heralded by rock and roll in the 1950s saw teenagers deserting the cinema for coffee bars and discotheques. This led to the arrival of clubbing as the main form of youth entertainment. Cinema going was no longer a young activity. It was in the suburbs that the decline was worst. Between 1955 and 1968 a total of 35 Nottingham cinemas closed, leaving just 11 in operation. A further six closed in the 1970s.[5]

The Carlton followed the Odeon's lead and was converted into three screens in December 1974. By 1977, the Odeon closed its Carola Restaurant in the lower ground floor, turning it into a further three screens, making a total of five.

52. Gala performance at Odeon One.

53. The Odeon closes down. October 2001.

The Savoy become three screens from July 1972, which may explain why of the many suburban cinemas this alone has survived; combined with the proximity of a large student population in its vicinity.

Finally, the arrival of multiplexes - the Showcase at Lenton in 1988 with 11 screens, and the Cine World on South Sherwood Street with 14 screens in 2001 brought about the end of the local cinema. The Odeon capitulated and was the last pre-war cinema to shut down in 2001.

Whilst the demolition of so many cinemas in the 50s and 60s was ruthless, it has to be remembered that such destruction was common throughout the country, frequently officially endorsed. The local authorities in Nottingham, which had encouraged the building of cinemas in the 1930s, showed indifference to their demise. This was the era in Nottingham when the removal of the Black Boy Hotel and the Collin's Almshouses on Friar Lane was approved by the City Council. Compared with this vandalism, the disappearance of cinemas was hardly noticed. Public reaction was mostly apathetic.

As late as 1981 the *Evening Post* reporting on the loss of the Beeston Astoria, noted that 'obviously the locals don't want to preserve the bizarre 1930s building.' [6]

This from the same newspaper which in 1936 when the Astoria was new had declared 'no more handsome cinema has yet to be seen in the Nottingham district'. [7]

54. The demolition of the Mechanics. Not only the loss of a cinema, but the hall where Dickens, Conan Doyle and Oscar Wilde had spoken.

Notes.
1. www.economicshelp.org
2. Ibid.
3. *Nottingham Local Studies.* Opening Programme for the Odeon Twin theatres, July 1965.
4. Ibid.
5. Sarah Stubbings: *From Modernity to Memorial.* Page 174. Nottm University PhD Thesis 2004.
6. *Nottingham Evening Post:* 5 May 1981.
7. *Nottingham Evening Post:* June 1936.

Modern Times

After the lowpoint of 1984, cinema attendance in this country has recovered and today stands at about 200 million admissions a year. Cinema going has changed, with separate performances now the norm. Of the many pre-war cinemas, the Savoy on Derby Road at Lenton continues valiantly as an independent. It had the foresight to convert itself into three screens in 1972 which may explain why of the many suburban cinemas this alone has survived; combined with the continual proximity of a large student population in its vicinity.

55. Cooper's original facade 1935.

56. The Savoy, sole survivor of the 1930s.

Otherwise multiplex cinemas have replaced the old locals and are situated either in the city centre or the outskirts such as Cine World on Sherwood Street, or the Showcase at Lenton, car ownership being almost essential for access to the latter. Restaurant and bar facilities are also available as valuable social amenities.

Nottingham today is fortunate in having Broadway one of the leading media centres in the country. In 1998, before its present incarnation, it was voted in the *Guardian* as one of the best independents in the country, with top marks for 'community vibe' and 'education facilities.'

Today, following a £5.7 million development in 2006, Broadway has four screens. Of these, Screen 4 created by Nottingham's eminent fashion designer Sir Paul Smith, has been chosen by *Total Film Magazine* as one of the ten best screens in the world.

Broadway has an environment that is 'unique yet comfortable without trying too hard.'[7]

56. *Cine World, Nottingham. 14 Screens under one roof.*

57. Broadway Media Centre,
Broad Street, Nottingham.

58. The Paul Smith Screen 4, Broadway.

Here can be seen first-run films, together with a cafe and two bars open most of the day. In addition there are regular relays by satellite from both the Royal Shakespeare Company, the National Theatre and the New York Metropolitan Opera. as well as numerous courses in film study. It is a place that invites - which has always been the aim of a successful cinema.

Film itself is now almost extinct. A modern feature film (the name still lingers) is in the form of a DVD or Blu-ray disc, the size of a paperback, and is shown by a DCP projector which is controlled by a touch screen. Broadway still has the facility to show 35mm film, as older films which are part of their programme have not always been converted to a digital format.

Yet for those who remember the old picture palaces it is not quite the same. We recall the magic of the moving beams of smoke filled light from the projection booth to the screen. The sound of the cinema organ, the communal experience of queuing and the double feature. Film historian David Thomson captures it well - 'Nothing in life in those first years after the war felt as good as being at the movies...Movies gave comfort and company at the same time...the dark that was an alternative to the harsh painful light outside.' [2]

Notes.
1. Guardian: 24 July 2012.
2. David Thomson: *The Whole Equation*. Little Brown, 2005.

Gazetteer of Nottingham Cinemas

It is difficult to be accurate on dates, changes of names and alterations. Every effort has been made to be correct, but inevitably some information may not be exact.

ACADEMY Picture House. Burton Street. Mechanics Institute Small Hall, Opened Nov.1909. Closed Jan. 1910. Demolished with the rest of the institute in 1964.

ADELPHI. Hucknall Lane, Bulwell. Architect: Reginald Cooper. 1,322 seats. Opened Feb.1937. Closed Dec. 1963. Demolished

APOLLO. See Berridge Road Picture House.

ASPLEY. Nuthall Road. aka Commodore.
1,294 seats. Stage 56′ x 25′ (17m x 7.62m). Opened Dec. 1932 by the Duchess of Portland. Closed Mar. 1956. Became Commodore Aug. 1956 - June 1958. Claimed to have biggest screen outside London. Demolished. Site now Sainsburys supermarket..

ASTORIA. Derby Road, Lenton Abbey. aka Essoldo / Classic. Architect: Alfred J. Thraves. 1,250 seats. Opened June 1936. *Evening Post* wrote 'No more handsome cinema has yet to be built in the Nottm. district.' From Aug.1952 owned by Essoldo Circuit. Later, Apr. 1972, owned by Classic Cinemas. Closed Oct.1975. Demolished.

BEESTON ESSOLDO. Station Road / Queens Road. aka Majestic. 1,038 seats.
Architect: E.S.Roberts. Opened as Majestic Sep.1938. Became Essoldo Aug.1952. Closed Sep. 1968. Demolished June 1988.

BERRIDGE ROAD PICTURE HOUSE. aka Apollo. 1,000 seats. Opened Mar. 1920. Renamed Apollo Mar. 1948. Closed Dec. 1960. In use as a mosque.

BONINGTON. Nottingham Road, Arnold.
900 seats. Opened as St Alban's Picturedrome Feb.1912. Closed Dec. 1929 to be reopened as Bonington Jan. 1930. Closed May 1957. Demolished.

BOULEVARD. Radford Road, Hyson Green. aka Electric Palace / New Boulevard.
Opened Dec. 1910. One of Nottingham's first suburban cinemas with silent films accompanied by ladies' orchestra. Closed May 1956. Demolished.

BRIDGFORD TUDOR. Tudor Square, West Bridgford. Architect: A.J. Thraves.
1, 391 Seats. Opened Sep. 1931. Closed Oct. 1959. Demolished.

BROADWAY. Broad Street. Nottingham Media Centre. Former Weslyan Chapel. Opened 24 Sep.1957 as Nottingham & District Film Society.
In 1959 merged with Nottingham Co-op Film Society.
In Sep.1966 became Nottingham Film Theatre with BFI sponsorship.
Aug.1989 became Broadway Cinema with Screen 1(534 seats) and Screen 2 (155 seats). Architects 1993,1997 Burrell Foley & Fischer.   Refurbished and reopened Oct. 2006 with addition of Screen 3 (100 seats) and Screen 4 (designed by regular patron Sir Paul Smith - 80 seats). In operation.

CAPITOL. Alfreton Road / Churchfield Lane, Radford. Architect: Reginald W. Cooper. Opened Oct. 1936. Closed June 1968. Listed grade II. In use as Mount Zion Millenium Church.

CARLTON. Chapel Bar / Mount St. aka ABC / Cannon / MGM. Architect: W.R.Glen.
2,077 seats. Proprietors Associated British Cinemas Ltd. Main rival to Odeon. Opened Oct. 1939. Converted to three screens Nov/ Dec. 1974. Taken over by Cannon 1986. Closed July 1999. Demolished.

CAVENDISH. St. Ann's Wells Road.
1,850 seats. Opened Aug.1938 by Mayoress and Googie Withers, star of first film *Convict 99*. Closed Sep.1968. In use as discount store.

CINE WORLD. South Sherwood Street. aka UCH / Warner Village / Corner House. Opened 2001. 14 Screens. Part of Cine World Group plc with 79 cinemas in the U.K. In operation.

COMMODORE. See Aspley.

COSY. See Netherfield Cosy.

CURZON. Mansfield Road, Carrington. Architect: C. Edmund Wilford. Opened Aug.1935. Closed Dec. 1958. Demolished.

DALE. Sneinton Dale. Architect: Alfred J. Thraves.
1,240 seats. (No balcony). Opened Dec.1932. Closed Apr. 1957. Demolished.

ELECTRA / ELECTRA HOUSE. See Orion.

ELITE. Parliament Street. Architect: Adamson & Kinns. Grade II listed (Exterior only).
1,477 seats. Opened Aug. 1921. In its day one of the most advanced cinemas in the UK. Contained three large cafes. 'one has the latest model

soda fountain, another designed as a ballroom.' Closed Apr 1977. Ground floor In use as a nightclub and shops.

EMPRESS. See New Empress.

ESSOLDO. See Beeston Essoldo.

FORUM. Aspley Lane. Architect: Alfred J. Thraves.
1,232 seats. Opened Feb.1937. Closed Apr.1959.

FUTURIST. Valley Road, Basford. Architect: Alfred J. Thraves.
1,000 seats. Opened July 1937. Remodelled and re-opened Dec. 1966.
Re-opened (Balcony only) Dec. 1976. Closed Aug. 1977.
In use as commercial premises.

GAUMONT. Sited between Wollaton Street and Goldsmith Street. aka Hippodrome. Architect: Bertie Crewe. 1,724 seats. Variety Theatre from Sep.1908 - Oct. 1927.
Re-opened as cinema Nov. 1927. Renamed Gaumont Feb. 1947.
Closed Jan. 1971. Demolished Feb. 1973.

GLOBE. Trent Bridge.
850 Seats. Opened Jan.1914. With arrival of sound seating, reduced to 684. Closed June 1961. Demolished.

GRAND. Radford Road, Hyson Green. aka Nottingham Repertory Theatre. Opened Feb.1886 as Theatre. Showed early bioscope films. By 1911 'showing world's best moving pictures as variety turns.' 1920-1923 known as Compton Repertory Theatre.
Full time cinema from 1926 onwards. Closed Sep.1956.
Demolished.

GROVE. Kirk White Street. Architect: Reginald W. Cooper.
780 seats. Opened July 1938. Closed Dec. 1962. Demolished.

HIBBERT'S. See Lounge Picture Theatre.

HIGHBURY. Highbury Vale, Bulwell.
1,100 seats. Opened Dec. 1921. Closed Mar. 1962. Demolished.

HIPPODROME. See Gaumont.

ILKESTON ROAD PICTURE HOUSE.
920 seats. Opened Nov. 1914. Closed Dec. 1962.

IMPERIAL PICTURE HOUSE. Wilford Road.
1,000 seats. Opened Sep. 1916. Enlarged By Alfred J. Thraves in 1937.
Damaged by floods 1947. Closed Jun 1957. Demolished.

KINEMA. Haydn Road, Sherwood. 800 seats. Opened Aug. 1913. Closed
Mar. 1941. In use as commercial premises.

KING'S Front Street, Arnold. aka Empress. 800 seats. Opened May 1913.
Became King's 1934. Closed Dec. 1947. Demolished.

LENO'S. Radford Road.
1,000 seats. Opened as Little John 1911 - 1912. Became Leno's (named
after Music Hall comedian Dan Leno) 1912. Closed 1968. Demolished.

LONG ROW PICTURE HOUSE. See Picture House.

LOUNGE PICTURE HOUSE. Shakespeare Street.
Nottingham's first cinema. Previously Central Christadelphian Hall.

Opened as Hibbert's Pictures Mar. 1910. Renamed Lounge Mar. 1920. Closed Sep.1937. Demolished.

MAJESTIC BEESTON. See Beeston Essoldo.

MAPPERLEY MAJESTIC. Woodborough Road. Architect: Alfred J. Thraves.
721 seats. Opened June 1929 by Councillor J.Farr. Described as 'Elite of the suburbs.' Closed Nov. / Dec. 1957. Became golf shop. Empty at present.

MECHANICS. Milton Street.
1,200 seats. Opened as Institute 1845. Damaged by fire 1867. Restored 1869. At one time the leading hall in city for lectures and concerts. Full time cinema from March 1916. Controlled by Gaumont-British from 1947. Closed June 1964. Demolished.

METROPOLE. Mansfield Road, Sherwood. Architect: Reginald W. Cooper.
1,600 seats. Opened Aug. 1937. 'Nottingham's largest suburban cinema.' Acquired by ABC circuit in 1943. Closed Oct. 1973. Demolished.

NEW BOULEVARD. See Boulevard.

NETHERFIELD COSY. Wright Street, Netherfield. aka Alexandra Picture Palace / Victoria Picture Palace. 550 seats. Opened July 1911. Same management as Kinema, Sherwood. Known as Cosy by 1933. Closed Apr. 1955. In use as commercial premises.

NEW EMPRESS. aka Empress. St. Ann's Wells Road.
1,491 Seats at one level. Former roller skating rink. Opened as Empress Jan. 1913. Reconstructed by architect Alfred J. Thraves and became New Empress Oct. 1928. Acquired by ABC circuit in 1941. Closed Nov. 1960. Demolished.

NEWS HOUSE. Entrances on both Parliament St. and Wollaton St. aka Parliament Street Picture House. 600 seats. Various name changes 1931 - 1935 e.g. Regal / British Cinema. Opened as News House July 1935. Renamed Odd Hour Cinema 1956. Closed Apr. 1957. Demolished.

ODEON. Angel Row. aka Ritz. Architects: Verity & Beverley with A.J.Thraves. 2,426 seats.
Nottingham's premier cinema. Opened Dec. 1933 as the Ritz. Became Odeon May 1944. First cinema in Britain to be 'twinned' by the Rank Organisation July 1965. Converted to 5 screens between Feb.1977 and 1988. Closed Jan. 2001. Demolished 2013.

ORION. Alfreton Road, aka Electra / Electra House. 800 seats. Opened May 1913. Closed Apr. 1959. Demolished.

PALACE. High Road, Beeston.
Opened Sept. 1912. Modernised and enlarged by Reginald T. Cooper and reopened in Sept. 1935. Closed Feb. 1960. Demolished.

PALACE THEATRE. Sneinton Road. aka Sneinton Picture Palace. 700 seats. Opened mid 1913. Closed Dec. 1945. Demolished.

PICTURE HOUSE. Long Row.
600 seats. Opened by Mayoress Nov. 1912. This was Nottingham's leading cinema until the Elite arrived (1921). Never converted to sound.

Closed Jan. 1930.
Facade grade II listed 1992. Became Lyons Tea Shop. Ground floor In use by Ladbrokes.

PICTURE PALACE. Main Street, Bulwell.
800 seats. Opened Nov. 1911. Closed mid 1950s. Demolished.

PLAZA. Trent Bridge. aka Pavilion / Pavilion Pictures / Palace.
Built on site of 1903 Midland International Exhibition.
(Destroyed by fire May 1904).
Opened May 1915 for concert parties. Opened Dec .1918 as Pavilion Picture House & Gardens. Re-styled by Alfred J. Thraves and reopened in May 1932 as Plaza.
Closed Mar. 1942. Demolished.

PRINGLE'S PICTURE PALACE. Goldsmith Street.
700 seats. Opened Nov. 1910. Closed as cinema Oct. 1941. Period as Nottingham Repertory Theatre / Little Theatre up to 1947. Became first Nottingham Playhouse Nov.1948 - July 1963. In use as night club.

QUEENS. Arkwright Street. aka Midlands Electric Picture Palace. 400 seats
Opened Dec. 1911. Closed June 1935 probably due to death of owner. Reopened as Queens Jan. 1936. Closed Jan. 1955. Demolished.

REGENT. Mansfield Road. aka Regent Hall.
900 seats. By 1915 showed films on week days and used on Sundays as a Baptist Tabernacle. In 1940 had 630 seats on the first floor, with balcony above. Closed by Fire Department Feb. 1941. Demolished.

RIO. Oakdale Road, Carlton. Architect: Reginald W. Cooper.
Opened Nov. 1939. (Delayed by outbreak of war). Closed Nov. 1959.
In use as a Food Hall.

RITZ. See Odeon.

RITZ CARLTON. Burton Road, Carlton. Architect: Reginald W. Cooper.
911 seats. Opened June 1936. Closed June 1968.

ROBIN HOOD PICTURE PALACE. St Ann's Wells Road.
500 seats. Opened April 1911. Closed Jan. 1932. Never converted to
'talkies.'

ROXY. Ribblesdale Road, Daybrook. Architect: Reginald W. Cooper.
1,100 seats. Opened Feb. 1937. Closed Nov. 1960. Demolished.

SAVOY. Derby Road, Lenton. Architect: Reginald W. Cooper.
1.300 seats. Opened Nov. 1935. Frontage remodelled by Cooper 1968.
Triple Screen from July1972. Remarkable for being the only 1930s cinema
still operating.

SCALA. Market Street.
Opened 1876 as Music Hall. Various changes of name. Talbot / Gaiety /
Kings in 1901 when films were first shown as variety turns.
Opened as Scala cinema Mar. 1913. 1,000 seats. Closed Apr. 1964.
Following periods as News and Cartoon Cinema until 1967. In 1969
twinned as Classic 1 and 2. Closed 1984. Demolished by 1991.

SCREEN ROOM. Broad Street. 21 seats. Claimed to be the smallest
cinema in the world. Opened 2002 and closed Dec. 2010. At present
empty.

SHOWCASE. Redfield Way, Lenton.
3,300 seats. Opened June 1988. 11 screens. Reputed at the time to be the largest showcase in UK. In operation.

TUDOR. See Bridgford Tudor.

VERNON. Vernon Road, Old Basford. aka Vernon Road Picture House. Opened Jan. 1917. Closed Sep. 1961. In use as commercial premises.

VICTORIA. Milton Street. aka Victoria Electric / New Victoria / Cine Moulin Rouge. Nottingham's first purpose-built cinema.
700 seats. Opened Mar. 1910. Became New Victoria Dec. 1949. Renamed Cine Moulin Rouge Dec. 1960. Closed Feb. 1970. Demolished.

WINDSOR. Hartley Road., Radford.
Opened June 1939. Closed June 1963. In use as carpet warehouse.

* * *

In addition to Nottingham Cinemas

Reginald W.G. Cooper also designed - Palladium, Ripon 1936. Ritz, Ilkeston 1938 (still standing now Grade II listed.) Regal, Stavely 1938. Metropole Westcliffe-on-Sea 1939.

Alfred J. Thraves also designed - Plaza, Mansfield 1930. King's, Sutton in Ashfield 1932. Parade, Skegness 1933. Byron, Hucknall 1936. Savoy, Spalding 1937. Gloria, Derby 1938.

Bibliography

Hamilton-Knight, Martine: *One City, One Hundred Years*. (Nottm. 1997.)

Hornsey, Brian: *Ninety years of Cinema in Nottingham*. (Mercia 1993. Updated 2001.)

Iliffe, Richard & Baguley Wilfred: *Victorian Nottingham,* Volume Three (Nottm. 1971.)
Edwardian Nottingham. Volume Two (Nottm.1980.)

Stubbings, Sarah BA, MA, *From Modernity to Memorial, The Changing Meaning of the 1930s Cinema in Nottingham*. (Thesis submitted to the University of Nottingham, August 2003.)

Thomson, David: *The Whole Equation*. (Little Brown 2005.)

Opening Brochure of Elite Cinema, 22 August 1921. (Nottingham Local Studies).

Opening Brochure of Ritz Cinema, 4 December 1933. (Nottingham Local Studies).

Opening Brochure of Twin Odeons, 12 July 1965. (Nottingham Local Studies).

Website: Cinema Treasures. org.

* * *

The Jazz Singer. The first talking picture, 1927.

At one time there were more than forty cinemas in Nottingham, offering continuous performances of films to huge audiences.

Going to the Pictures tells the story of these Picture Palaces, from their beginning, as side shows at Goose Fair, to the present day Mulitiplexes and Media Centres. Included are photographs of many lost cinemas and memorabilia connected with them.

£4.99

ISBN 978-1-902443-12-6

9 781902 443126